The
CALDER & HEBBLE
NAVIGATION

Horse-drawn wooden craft were the mainstay of the Calder & Hebble Navigation for much of its commercial lifetime and most carrying companies owned horses which were based at various points on the waterway. The Calder &Hebble Navigation Company maintained stables at several locations and, in addition, stables were provided by several pubs, such as the Navigation and the Jolly Sailor at Wakefield. Here, a horse with its handler and a 57ft 6in x 14ft 2in (West Country size) wooden vessel, its captain, his wife and son standing at the stern, pose for the photographer in the 1900s as it leaves the upper one of Double Locks at Thornhill, near Dewsbury. Most horses used were either mares or geldings of about fifteen hands (approximately 5ft high) and were usually crossbred Shire types aged five to twelve years, although older animals were frequently worked. The horse line trailing over the barge's bows and into the water is attached to the animal and will become taut as it takes up the strain, and passage along Long Cut begins. The vessel is loaded with about seventy-five tons of coal, extension boards having been fitted to the coamings in order to increase its carrying capacity. The lock-keeper's house and the Normanton to Hebden Bridge part of the Leeds & Manchester Company's railway line, opened in 1840, are visible in the background and both are still in existence today.

The
CALDER & HEBBLE
NAVIGATION

Mike Taylor

TEMPUS

John Smeaton (1724-1792) Britain's first professional
engineer, was requested to survey a route for the
Calder & Hebble Navigation and his findings were
published in 1757. After completing work on
Eddystone Lighthouse in 1759, he was employed as
Consulting Engineer on the waterway until replaced by
James Brindley for one year in 1765. Upon Smeaton's
return in 1766, his assistant, the young William Jessop,
played an increasingly important role as the Calder &
Hebble Navigation reached completion.

First published 2002
Copyright © Mike Taylor, 2002

Tempus Publishing Limited
The Mill, Brimscombe Port,
Stroud, Gloucestershire, GL5 2QG
www.tempus-publishing.com

ISBN 0 7524 2755 5

TYPESETTING AND ORIGINATION BY
Tempus Publishing Limited
PRINTED IN GREAT BRITAIN BY
Midway Colour Print, Wiltshire

Contents

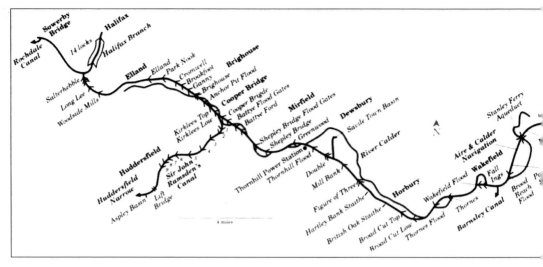

A map of the Calder & Hebble Navigation of the early twentieth century, showing its junctions with adjoining waterways.

Acknowledgements

I have learned about the Calder & Hebble Navigation from men who worked on the waterway in the first half of the twentieth century. Many of them are now deceased, including Edward Clegg of the Clegg Brothers, Reggie Wood, son of Albert Wood, Billy and Ernest Oates who crewed Duttons' craft and Ken Kettle, a former Calder Carrying Co. captain, all of whom gave freely of their time, knowledge and opinions. During the preparation of this book, Douglas Carey, another ex-Calder Carrying Co. boatman who moved to Hargreaves on nationalisation in 1948 like most of the aforementioned, showed great interest in the project and has been most helpful in imparting his knowledge and answering my many questions. Similarly, Arthur Millard, who began work on the Calder & Hebble Navigation in 1944, has also given considerable assistance. Peter Spence has kindly shared his knowledge of the Halifax Branch with me and, generally, the text owes something to material, including standard reference books such as Charles Hadfield's *Canals of Yorkshire and North East England*, made readily available by the Waterways Museum at Goole.

My thanks are also due to all the providers of photographs, several of which were given to me by the men named above. Those taken by the late Peter Smith have added greatly to the book, and Trevor Ellis, John Goodchild, Miss C. Humpleby, David Shepherd of Hargreaves and Peter Spence have all kindly allowed me access to their collections.

Introduction

The River Calder rises in the Pennines north of Todmorden and flows generally east through a deep and rugged valley to Sowerby Bridge and beyond Salterhebble where it receives the Hebble Brook, a small fast-flowing stream which skirts the north and east of Halifax on the way from its source at Ovenden. The augmented Calder then passes through Elland, Brighouse, Mirfield and Dewsbury before reaching Wakefield, becoming part of the Aire & Calder Navigation Co.'s (A&CNC) waterway before it is absorbed by the River Aire at Castleford.

Interest in making the Calder navigable further inland developed after the Aire & Calder had made Wakefield accessible in 1702. John Smeaton eventually surveyed a route and the relevant Act was passed in 1758. Smeaton also superintended construction and, by the early 1770s, the Company of Proprietors of the Calder & Hebble Navigation (C&HNC) had a waterway between Wakefield and Sowerby Bridge that was open for traffic. It comprised 21% canal cuts with the rest of the river and was able to accommodate craft up to twenty-five tons capacity. The navigation flourished when, in 1804, the Rochdale Canal was opened, crossing the Pennines from Sowerby Bridge and completing the first Humber-Mersey wide boat link, though the Trent & Mersey Canal had afforded a circuitous east-west link for narrow boats when it opened twenty-seven years earlier. A third route from the North Sea to the Irish Sea was provided in 1811, with the completion of the Huddersfield Narrow Canal. Sir John Ramsden's Canal linked the Calder & Hebble at Cooper Bridge with Huddersfield, and had been opened thirty-five years earlier. A third trans-Pennine waterway, the Leeds & Liverpool Canal, which used the Aire & Calder to reach Leeds from the Humber ports, began carrying through cargoes in 1816 and did not involve the Calder & Hebble.

For nearly a century, the Calder & Hebble was efficiently operated from its Halifax head office. Some canal cuts were extended and new ones built to supersede existing ones by avoiding further sections of river, and the canal up to Halifax from Salterhebble was built. The present-day route, with 68% canal cuts and the ability to accommodate craft carrying up to seventy tons on its upper reaches and more below, had been established by the mid-nineteenth century. However, never as profitable as the neighbouring Aire & Calder, the Calder & Hebble was leased to the A&CNC for twenty-one years in the mid-nineteenth century. The only major event before nationalisation in 1948 was acquisition by the C&HNC of Huddersfield Broad (Sir John Ramsden's) Canal in 1944.

The maximum size of craft able to navigate the entire Calder & Hebble is 57ft 6in x 14ft 2in (described, probably initially by Humber-based boatmen, as 'West Country' size). Because locks on adjoining waterways were of different dimensions, cargoes often had to be transhipped from one vessel to another and Huddersfield, Sowerby Bridge and Wakefield saw much of this activity. Huddersfield Narrow locks had dimensions of 70ft x 7ft, those on the Rochdale were 74ft x 14ft 9in while Huddersfield Broad locks were 57ft 6in x 14ft 2in, like those on most of the Calder & Hebble. Locks on the Aire & Calder were bigger than any of these.

This book concentrates on the carriage of cargoes on the Calder & Hebble and adjoining waterways. Coal was the major cargo, brought to the waterside by wagonways and tramways at various points on the navigation, as well as being loaded directly at colliery staithes near Wakefield, both on the Calder & Hebble and Aire & Calder. The coal was then delivered to gasworks, power stations, mills and coal merchants on the Calder & Hebble and elsewhere. Wool, coir, jute, grain, flour and cocoa beans were collected from Hull, Goole or Grimsby docks and, together with cement loaded in Hull Harbour or South Ferriby, brought to Calder & Hebble wharves. Chemicals were carried to and from Dewsbury and Huddersfield, and stone from the quarries near Brighouse and Elland was exported in both directions.

At its peak in the mid-nineteenth century, the Calder & Hebble carried over half a million tons annually. By 1905, this had gradually declined to 465,000 tons, of which three-quarters were exchanged with the Aire & Calder, one-sixth used only the first mile above Wakefield and one third used only the first five miles at the eastern end of the navigation. The Halifax Branch handled 57,000 tons of the 1905 total and the Huddersfield Broad 64,000 tons, 11,000 tons of which went onto the Huddersfield Narrow. In 1975, when only the coal traffic to Thornhill Power Station remained, 127,000 tons were carried and this had fallen to 76,000 tons by 1980, the last full year of deliveries.

Until the 1930s, some Hull-based, West Country size vessels were fitted with sails, though craft owned by H. Mellor & Sons were almost the only Calder & Hebble-registered craft rigged for sailing. The rest were all tiller-steered wooden dumb boats. Most were usually hauled by a hired horse and horse marine on the Calder & Hebble, but this was an expensive option for private owners. Alternatively, the crew could bow haul the vessel or, if it was fitted with sails, they could sail up the navigation with an easterly wind or come down with a westerly. One captain's record for the eighteen miles between Elland and Wakefield was eight hours, involving passage through twenty-one locks and forty-six bridges, only three of which were high enough to sail under without lowering the mast. However, by the late 1930s Duttons' steam tug *Tybourne* and the Calder Carrying Co.'s diesel-engined towing barge *Frank W* were also working, and steel craft began to appear – notably as Hargreaves' motor barges *No.60* and *No.61* were introduced in 1938. Horse-haulage ended in 1953, the last wooden vessel was built at Mirfield in 1955 and steel craft were the exclusive carriers on the Calder & Hebble from the mid-1970s; older wooden vessels had been kept afloat by running them into mud on the canal bed and the use of ashes and sawdust kept aboard used to seal leaking seams. Tiller-steered vessels were converted to wheel steering by this time and wheelboxes had been fitted, while dumb craft had had engines installed. Craft carried about eighty tons on a draught of 6ft, sixty tons on the 5ft guaranteed up to Brighouse and about forty tons from above Brighouse to Huddersfield.

The commercial decline of the Calder & Hebble was accelerated after nationalisation as the BTC refurbished their depot at Wakefield and closed their other former A&CNC and C&HNC warehouses on the waterway. They then delivered cargoes bound for the Calder Valley by road from Wakefield, effectively killing off much of the barge activity on the waterway.

After Chapter 1, which gives a general overview of the Calder & Hebble, subsequent chapters consist of illustrations arranged in no chronological order, moving upstream from Wakefield with occasional relevant diversions, especially onto the Aire & Calder. Inevitably, though spanning a period of over a century, almost all photographs used date from the twentieth century with many appearing on postcards. My own photographs and those from my collection are uncredited, while other illustrations are acknowledged individually.

Chronology for the commercial history of the Calder & Hebble and associated waterways:

1702   Aire & Calder navigable to Wakefield from both Leeds and Knottingley. (Knottingley accessible for sea-going craft via River Aire).

1770   Calder & Hebble opened (twenty-two miles, twenty-eight locks, with a fall of 192 $\frac{1}{2}$ ft from Sowerby Bridge to Wakefield). Dewsbury had been reached in 1762 and Brighouse by 1764. Flooding around Salterhebble in 1767 and 1768 delayed completion to Sowerby Bridge.

1776   Huddersfield Broad Canal opened (four miles, nine locks, between Cooper Bridge and Huddersfield).

1804   Rochdale Canal opened (thirty-three miles, ninety-two locks, between Sowerby Bridge and Castlefield, Manchester).

1811   Huddersfield Narrow Canal opened (twenty miles, seventy-four locks, between Huddersfield and Ashton-under-Lyne).

1828   Halifax Branch of Calder & Hebble opened (1 $\frac{1}{2}$ miles, fourteen locks, between Salterhebble and Halifax).

1865   Calder & Hebble leased for twenty-one years by A&CNC who built or leased warehouses on Calder & Hebble over next few years. The company purchased derelict Savile Cut, near Dewsbury and lengthened some locks at eastern end.

1942   Halifax Branch abandoned.

1944   C&HNC purchased Huddersfield Broad Canal from LMS Railway as the Huddersfield Narrow Canal was abandoned.

1948   Calder & Hebble nationalised to be operated by British Transport Commission (BTC), eventually passing to the British Waterways Board (BW) in 1963. All warehouses on Calder & Hebble, except Wakefield, closed over next few years.

1952   Rochdale Canal abandoned.

1981   Regular commercial carrying on Calder & Hebble ended when British Oak-Thornhill power station traffic ceased.

One

General Characteristics

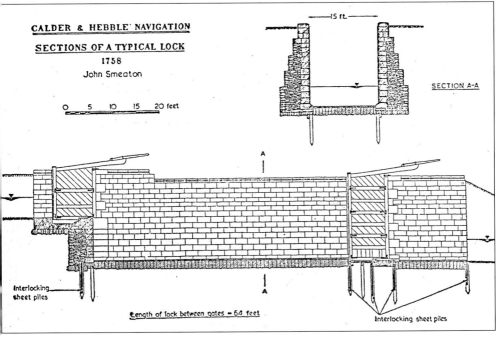

CALDER & HEBBLE NAVIGATION

SECTIONS OF A TYPICAL LOCK
1758
John Smeaton

SECTION A-A

As a river navigation, the Calder & Hebble comprised river sections and lock cuts. The latter were protected by flood gates at the upstream end as the river went over a nearby weir. Some cuts had intermediate standard-type locks along their length but a standard lock always facilitated cut/river transfers at their downstream end. The illustration shows Smeaton's original drawing for Millbank lock, near Thornhill.

The lock at the eastern end of Greenwood cut at Ravensthorpe, one of the original eighteenth century cuts, is here viewed from across the Calder in the 1920s. The lock-keeper's residence was demolished in 1971.

Floodgates at the western end of Greenwood cut are shown open. In the case of high river levels, the gates would be closed to keep excess water out of the cut (beneath the bridge). This effectively closed the navigation and cargoes were delayed. When the A&CNC leased the waterway, it changed some flood gates into flood locks so that craft could still enter or leave the top end of the cuts thus treated. Brighouse cargoes however were regularly delayed, as three sets of unchanged flood gates remained below the town on Cooper Bridge, Battyeford and Greenwood cuts.

This view from the flood lock at the top end of Mirfield cut shows the river passing over the weir in the 1970s. After a tragic incident at Cromwell Lock on the River Trent, weirs on the Calder & Hebble Navigation are now protected by a string of floats stretching across the river.

Occasionally on a river navigation, the towpath changes sides at the transition between lock cut and river section and provision had to be made for horses to cross. The Calder & Hebble had horse bridges at Brighouse (washed away in the 1940s), Mirfield (demolished c.1958; the bridge pier is visible in mid-river on the previous picture) and Battyeford (shown here with the river flowing from left to right). Described as a 'turnover' bridge, as there is no need to unhitch the towrope, a horse hauling a vessel upstream would cross the bridge and then come down the right-hand approach ramp before turning to pass beneath the arch. The bridge was extensively renovated a few years ago, but still retains its cobbled footway suitable for horses.

Where no bridges existed, horses had to be ferried across river, as here at the end of Long Cut. Ravensthorpe's Calder Wharf and Warehouse lay across the river as did the C&HNC's stables and towpath to wharves down river above Dewsbury. A horse is shown being brought across from the wharf in the 18ft long double-ended rowboat. This ferry service ended in the 1930s, though construction of a nearby road bridge in the late nineteenth century had made it redundant earlier. The ferry across the river from the flood lock at Wakefield Cut finished at about the same time, but the chain-operated horse ferry below Broad Cut bottom lock continued into the 1950s. Calder Warehouse still stands today, with windows in place of the hoist doors shown.

Opposite below: Part of the front cover of the C&HNC's 1938 publication promoting their waterway as an essential part of an east-west link.

A 3ft-long 'handspike' is used to operate ground paddles close to the top gates of several locks on the Calder & Hebble. The device is inserted into one of the sockets on a small iron wheel, which is then rotated by leverage. The toothed beam is thus raised and the paddles opened, allowing water to pass into the lock. Several of these distinctive devices still remain and two notable canal enthusiasts have combined to illustrate one in use. The late John Gagg, whose writings and photographs have attracted many readers to our inland waterways, took this picture of the late Ralph Kirkham, perhaps the Calder & Hebble's most lucid and vociferous advocate, manipulating the apparatus. John sent me the negative to print and agreed to its use in this book only two weeks before he died.

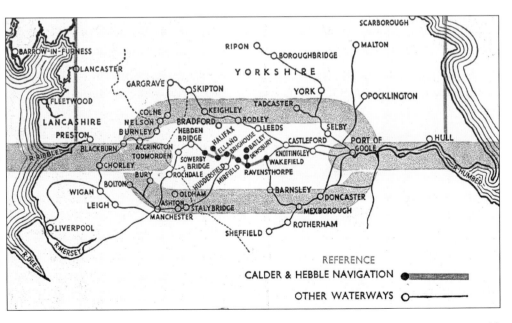

THE WATER LINK
FROM COAST TO COAST
(THE CALDER AND HEBBLE NAVIGATION)

THE Calder & Hebble Navigation was constructed under various Acts of Parliament from 1758 to 1834, and is an important link in the east to west coast system of Canals, as it joins the Aire & Calder Navigation at Fall Ing Lock, Wakefield (thus affording access to the east-coast ports of Goole, Hull, Grimsby and Immingham), and at the termination of the system at Sowerby Bridge, the Navigation joins the Rochdale Canal whose terminus is at Manchester, and they in turn connect with the Manchester Ship Canal Co., thus providing the necessary link with Liverpool and Runcorn. At Manchester there is also a junction with the Bridgewater Department of the Manchester Ship Canal.

At Double Locks, Thornhill, there is a Branch Canal to Savile Town, Dewsbury, belonging to the Aire & Calder Navigation; whilst at Cooper Bridge there is a junction to Huddersfield.

The main line of Canal is from Sowerby Bridge to Wakefield, with a Branch Canal from Salterhebble to Halifax. The total length of waterway owned by the Navigation is just over 27 miles, and during its comparatively short length it serves numerous important manufacturing and industrial towns of the West Riding, including Wakefield, Horbury, Thornhill, Ravensthorpe, Mirfield, Cooper Bridge, Brighouse, Elland, Halifax and Sowerby Bridge.

At Wakefield it is possible to deal with barges carrying up to 150 tons, and throughout the whole of the system boats can travel carrying at least 60 tons.

The C&HNC's description of its own waterway from the 1938 publication.

Despite the severe competition from other forms of transport, the Navigation continues to serve a useful purpose in dealing with heavy traffic of all description, and numerous improvements for the speedier handling of traffic are continually being effected.

Barges may receive goods from overside steamer at Hull, Goole, Liverpool or Manchester, and carry to destination, into customer's works, thus eliminating heavy landing charges.

A large amount of coal passes over the Navigation from the coal pits near Horbury, Wakefield, Barnsley and Castleford, and in many cases the traffic is discharged direct from barge to the boiler-house of factories.

Every encouragement is given to traders owning barges to work on the Navigation, and Through Toll arrangements are in operation with the adjoining Navigations, which enable a boat to load at, say, Hull, and travel to, say, Manchester, over three or more different Navigations on payment of one toll, which is collected by the first Navigation.

Canal transport during the past few years has been speeded up with the increasing numbers of mechanically-propelled barges.

From the foregoing it is hoped that the business man will give increased consideration to the question of making fuller use of the country's Silent Highways, which are the safest means of transporting all types of goods.

In addition, the management are always prepared to offer every possible assistance to firms to establish works alongside the Navigation, in order that they may take advantage to the full of the Navigation's facilities.

At the various wharves and warehouses throughout the system goods can be stored for customers, and delivered as required to destination, by the Navigation's own motor transport service.

Our final word is: Principals and Executives should hasten to acquaint themselves with the possible advantage and saving which here lie ready to hand.

CALDER CARRYING CO. LTD

LONDON OFFICE
2 & 4 ST. MARY AXE
LEADENHALL ST.,
E.C.3.
Tel. Avenue 1622

● *CANAL CARRIERS* of all classes of Merchandise between Hull and Goole to the densely populated districts of the West Riding of Yorkshire and Lancashire. Enquiries are welcomed and rates quoted.

GOOLE OFFICE
20 PERCY STREET

● *SHIPBUILDERS.* The Mirfield Dockyard is fully equipped with skilled labour and the most modern plant for supplying and repairing all types of Canal and River Craft from a Barge to a Rowing Boat. May we quote for your requirements ?

HULL OFFICE
21 HIGH STREET
Tel. Hull 16507

● *CONTINENTAL AGENCY.* Ask your Continental Suppliers to get the cheapest through rates from our Agents at Hamburg, for goods from any Continental Station to any point served by the Calder and Hebble Navigation.

HAMBURG
W. DIECKMANN
& Co.
NEUERWALL 70-74
HAMBURG, 36.
Tel. 348300

HEAD OFFICE
52 SOUTHGATE, HALIFAX Tel. HALIFAX 3964
General Manager: H. JACKSON, A.M.Inst.T.

Left: About 1900, the C&HNC formed the Calder Carrying Co. to move cargoes on its waterway in its own craft and this is a copy of an advertisement dating from the 1930s. On nationalisation in 1948, this company was taken over by Hargreaves (West Riding) and operated by them until it was wound up in 1953.

Below: Details of carrying companies using the Calder & Hebble, taken from the 1940s publication, *Handbook on Inland Waterways.*

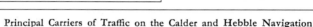

Principal Carriers of Traffic on the Calder and Hebble Navigation

NAME	ADDRESS	COMMODITY CARRIED
Acaster, T.	6, Jefferson Street, Goole	Coal, General Goods.
Askew, S.	26, Regent Street, Belle Vue, Wakefield	Coal.
Aire & Calder Navigation	Dock Street, Leeds, 1.	General Goods.
Barker, H.	186, Newtown Square, Hedon Road, Hull	General Goods.
Calder Carrying Co., Ltd.	Navigation House, Navigation Road, Halifax	General Goods, Coal.
Cawood, Wharton & Co., Ltd.	1, Cavendish Road, Leeds, 1	Coal.
Clay, T., & Sons	Chapel Lane, Sowerby Bridge	Coal.
Clegg, E. & J.	" Granview," Sowerby New Road, Sowerby Bridge.	Coal.
Cook, J. W., & Co. Ltd.	Temple Buildings, Bowlalley Lane, Hull	Petrol.
Dutton, W. (Exors. of)	Canal Wharf, Elland	Coal, General Goods.
Ellis, I.	Myrtle Cottage, Canal Bank, Salterhebble, Nr. Halifax.	Coal.
Fletcher, T., & Sons (Canal Transport) Ltd.	51, Salthouse Lane, Hull	Grain, Coal, General Goods.
Hall, J. H. (Exors. of)	Fitzwilliam Buildings, 104, Alfred Gelder Street, Hull.	Grain.
Harker, John, Ltd.	Knottingley	Petrol, Oil.
Hargreaves, J., & Sons (Leeds) Ltd.	The Calls, Leeds, 2	Coal.
Mellor, H., & Sons	Bradford Road, Brighouse	Grain, Coal.
Pilkington, J.	C/o Canal Wharf, Brighouse	Coal.
Poppleton, W. D., Ltd.	17A, Victoria Street, Huddersfield	Coal.
Rogerson, W.	233, Doncaster Road, Agbrigg, Wakefield	Coal.
Scargill, T. & W., Ltd.	Mill Street East, Savile Town, Dewsbury	Coal.
Shaw, A.	4, Oakenshaw Street, Agbrigg, Wakefield	Coal.
Shaw, G.	234, Barnsley Road, Sandal Croft, Wakefield	Coal.
Sugden, T., & Sons Ltd.	Brighouse	Grain.
Thornton, Hannam & Marshall Ltd.	Brookfoot Dyeworks, Brighouse	Coal.
Whittles, G. W.	81, Brindley Street, East Park, Hull	General Goods.
Wilby, James, Ltd.	Ropergate, Pontefract	Coal.
Yorkshire Tar Distillers Ltd.	Whitechapel Lane, Cleckheaton	Tar.

Hargreaves Industrial Services Ltd, originally named James Hargreaves & Sons (Leeds) Ltd, first started operating on the Calder & Hebble with hired barges in 1933, carrying coal to the Yorkshire Electric Power Company's Thornhill Power Station.

In 1938 they had the first two of their own 'West Country' barges no's 60 and 61, built at John Harkers Ltd, Knottingley.

With the coming of World War II in 1939, expansion was restricted and it was not until after the war, in 1946, that the company had its next two West County boats, Marjorie R and Renee built. Expansion in canal transport on the navigation then followed quite rapidly by the acquisition in the late 1940's and early 1950's, of a number of canal carriers on the Calder & Hebble. These included I. & J. Dutton who were engaged principally in carrying coal to Thornhill Power Station, the Calder Carrying Co. Ltd., Thomas Clay & Sons, W. D. Poppleton Ltd.

With the takeover of Calder Carrying Co. Ltd., Hargreaves also acquired Ledgard Bridge Dockyard at Mirfield where they continued to build one wooden West Country barge each year from 1948 to 1955. All but one of the newly-built vessels were added to Hargreaves own fleet and used on their coal carrying operations which at that time included coal from Water Haigh, Whitwood, West Riding, Parkhill and British Oak and Hartley Bank collieries to such destinations as Thornhill and Huddersfield Power Stations, Sowerby Bridge and Elland Gas Works, Brighouse Wharf, B.D.A. at Brookfoot.

Regrettably, over the years, various factors such as the building of the big new gas works at Tingley, colliery closures, cheap oil, natural gas and the restrictive dimensions of the waterway, which prevented canal transport improving its competitiveness as road and rail were able to do, took their toll until today the coal tonnage from British Oak to Thornhill Power Atation, is the only remaining commercial traffic on the Calder & Hebble navigation.

New vessels were built, but older worn out ones were scrapped over the years and by 1975 the last of the wooden barges had been phased out and replaced so far as needed and available by second-hand steel barges. The fleet was now reduced from some 30 barges in its heyday to only eight steel barges, seven of these are still in use on the Calder and Hebble, the eighth now being used as power unit for loading compartment barges in a colliery basin. Of the seven remaining, No. 61, Marjorie R and Renee still soldier on.

In 1979, when Thornhill power station had been receiving coal by water for seventy-five years, Hargreaves prepared this display notice. Mellors, Sugdens and the Bradford Dyers' Association were the respective owners of three of the few barge fleets that were not taken over by Hargreaves. For a short period of its existence, Hargreaves' fleet carried cargoes other than coal.

West Country motor vessels owned by Hargreaves (West Riding) in 1948, after Nationalisation. Building dates in brackets.

Owned by Hargreaves from new; *No 60* (1938), *No 61* (1938), *Renee* (1946) and *Marjorie R* (1946). All four craft were built of steel by Harkers of Knottingley.

Ex-Calder Carrying Company; *Brighouse* [ex-*Mildred*] (1909), *Ravensthorpe* [ex-*Esther*] (1909), *Wakefield* [ex-*Joseph*] (1914), *Salterhebble* [ex-*Thomas*] (1916), *Horbury* [ex-*Margaret Mary*] (1921), *Elland* [ex-*John*] (1921), *Wakefield* [ex-*Peter*] (1924), *Cooper Bridge* [ex-*Robert*] (1934), *Frank W* (1937), *Sowerby Bridge* (1943) and *Brookfoot* (1945). All were wooden craft, most built at Mirfield, some as dumb craft, motorised before the end of World War II. Names were changed to C&HN locations as an aid to recognition of vessels by naval patrols in the Humber during World War II.

ex-Duttons; *Primrose* (1916), *Yeponian* (1934), *Regal* (1935), *Excelsior* (1939) and *Frugality* (1940).

List of Hargreaves' vessels.

The prize for BBC television's *Blue Peter* competition winners was a tour of the Yorkshire coalfield, and they are pictured here with barge captain Ken Kettle on Hargreaves' *No.61* at British Oak staithe as a vessel coming to load winds further up the canal.

Two
Wakefield
(Fall Ings Cut)

The Calder & Hebble begins at Fall Ings lock, Wakefield, out of sight beneath the footbridge arch on this photograph from the 1920s. Taken from the opposite bank of the river, it shows the A&CNC's towing barge, *No. 10*, which has probably brought dumb barges loaded at Hull or Goole up the navigation and is waiting to collect vessels to be towed back down the waterway.

An unladen A&CNC dumb boat waiting below Fall Ings lock for a tow downriver. The vessel is probably one of the three West Country 'flyboats' built in 1868 by the A&CNC especially for the Calder trade. The horse grazing amongst the hens would probably have towed the vessel down the Calder & Hebble from Dewsbury, Halifax or Huddersfield. As late as the early 1950s, after nationalisation, the BTC had a horse based at Wakefield for towage up to Broad Cut and another based at Dewsbury for towage from Broad Cut to either Dewsbury or Huddersfield.

The vessels shown were photographed in the 1920s, moored outside E. Green & Son's economiser works on a former arm of the Aire & Calder, below Wakefield weir. In the 1910s, '20s and '30s, *Esther* (nearer the camera) and *Mildred* were used to ship their products to Salford Docks via the Calder & Hebble and the Rochdale canals, as well as to Hull Docks. The craft were subsequently sold to the Calder Carrying Co. who motorised and then renamed them. (*John Goodchild Collection*)

Hargreaves' West Country size motor boat, *No.61*, leaving Fall Ings lock in the 1960s with a cargo of coal for Ferrybridge power station on the Aire & Calder. The photograph was taken by the late Peter Smith who was responsible for many of the illustrations in this book. *(P.L. Smith)*

The footbridge over Fall Ings lock had been replaced by a less attractive structure by the time the motor vessel *Saira* was photographed passing onto the Calder & Hebble carrying jute, coir, wool or other low density cargo in the 1960s. Fall Ings cut was rerouted in 1812 and its single lock, opened in 1761, replaced by two locks. In 1882, these two locks were converted into the one of 130ft x 22ft shown here, thus enabling larger craft using the Aire & Calder to have access to wharves on the Calder & Hebble at Wakefield and reducing the number of locks on the Calder & Hebble to twenty-seven. *(P.L. Smith)*

Cawoods Hargreaves began delivering coal to Ferrybridge C power station using push-towed pans in 1967. The coal was collected from several staithes and here, in 1971, two pans loaded on the Calder & Hebble have been photographed from the footbridge over Fall Ings lock as they are manhandled into position for penning down. The lockhouse formerly stood on the ground to the right until its demolition in 1967. (*P.L. Smith*)

A lorry-fed coal staithe was built in Fall Ings cut and the first cargo was loaded here in March 1939. A Leeds & Liverpool Canal shortboat is shown waiting to receive that cargo.

Predecessors of the Cawoods Hargreaves pans were the compartment boats or Tom Puddings, dating from the mid-nineteenth century. In another photograph taken from the footbridge over the lock in 1965, compartments loaded at the nearby Fall Ings staithe wait to be collected for haulage to Goole. Huge tonnages were exported by this means from several waterside collieries in West Riding. (*P.L. Smith*)

A train of loaded compartments bound for Goole is shown heading along the Wakefield Branch of the Aire & Calder behind a steam tug early in the twentieth century. The 'jebus' between the tug and train of puddings lifted the leading compartments and deflected the tug's wash beneath the vessels.

On arrival at Goole, contents of the compartments were tipped into ships' holds using one of these distinctive hoists on the dock estate. When the compartment boats ceased to operate in the mid-1980s, they had carried over fifty-five million tons of solid fuel in 122 years. Much of it was exported to near-European ports, but considerable amounts were taken to English south and east-coast destinations as well as to River Thames gasworks.

For several years coal from Hartley Bank Colliery was carried to Earles, the cement maufacturers up the harbour at Hull. *Evelynston* is shown moored overnight within Fall Ings flood lock in 1963 while en route for the River Hull. Hatches and covers are in place, a necessary precaution for a voyage on the sometimes rough River Humber. The traffic ended in 1967. (*P.L. Smith*)

Above: Situated on the 'corner' formed by the River Calder and the upper end of Fall Ings cut lay the BTC warehouse where one of their motor barges is shown discharging a cargo in the 1950s. At this time, at least five barges per week arrived here bringing goods loaded at one of the Humber Ports.

Right: Two dumb barges hauled by an out-of-shot tug or motor barge, are seen carrying coal past the BTC depot at Wakefield as they head along the cut towards Fall Ings lock in the early 1950s. The wooden canopy sheltering berths outside the warehouse was removed a few years later and the warehouse itself replaced by one of corrugated iron construction.

Hargreaves' diesel tug, *Elsa Margareta*, is shown hauling two of their coal-filled dumb vessels into Wakefield cut through the top gates of the flood lock, bound for one of the Ferrybridge power stations. Part of the new warehouse is visible to the right of this picture, dating from the late 1950s. (*P.L. Smith*)

A fuller view of the new warehouse built in the mid-1950s showing the former canopy support 'island' to the left. *Waterdog B.W.*, the motor vessel discharging a cargo in 1961, was formerly the Aire & Calder's *No.81*, a 90ft x 17ft dumb barge.

Three
Wakefield Pond

A view of the 1950s-built warehouse just downstream from the flood lock leading into Fall Ings cut. The photograph was taken from across the Calder and also shows part of the old A&CNC warehouse to the left. *Valour B.W.* is discharging a similar cargo to the one that *Saira* was carrying in the photograph on page 21. The depot was closed in 1982, having been served by road since 1974 when it received its final delivery by barge.

Sacks of flour destined for a wharf on the Calder & Hebble are being transhipped from the outer sailing sloop into the inner West Country size vessel outside the old A&CNC warehouse at Wakefield, on this photograph from the 1920s. There were also facilities for transhipment on the riverside upstream of the entrance to Fall Ings cut.

Featuring Wakefield weir, responsible for maintaining a navigable depth in the 'pond' but originally constructed in the thirteenth century to provide water power for nearby mills, this advertising card highlights the two water-served mills owned by Reynolds, Stott & Haselgrave in the 1900s.

Opposite below: A crowd has collected to watch the launch of a wooden keel in 1900. The boatyard is probably on the south bank of the Calder, close to Wakefield weir.

In this picture, artistic licence seems to have brought the two mills shown in the previous picture closer together than they were in reality. The drawing dates from the mid-nineteenth century when Wakefield was the administrative centre of Yorkshire's West Riding and was also home to the north of England's largest corn market. Vessels, including sea-going craft shown, brought imported foreign grain as well as the produce of Lincolnshire and East Anglia to the market, which reached its height of prosperity in 1870. Smaller craft then often carried it further up the Calder & Hebble and often over the Pennines via the Rochdale Canal. (*John Goodchild Collection*)

In 1933, a new and wider road bridge was built diagonally across Wakefield weir, necessitating the demolition of King's Mill and bypassing the chantry chapel visible on both this and the picture on page 29.

One of T. Fletcher & Sons steam keels discharging a cargo of grain at West Riding mill in the 1930s. This company continued to bring grain here until 1968, after the mill had been demolished. It was then carried by road further into the Calder Valley.

Blundy, Clark & Co. of York had three craft torn from their moorings in Wakefield by high winds in December 1951. A flooding river then took them from Thornes Lane wharf and over the weir; a not uncommon problem on river navigations. The motor barge *Henrietta* stayed close to the weir as shown on this snapshot, dumb barge *Kate* (nearest the camera) was swept onto the bank and *Saira*, the other dumb barge involved, came to rest beneath the bridge arch. They were all recovered by being pulled beneath the two bridges.

Imported grain was often stored in the silo at the end of Hull's King George Dock before being transferred to barge for delivery onto the Calder & Hebble and other inland waterways. Sometimes the grain was loaded directly overside from ships and here, in Hull's King George dock, *Middlesex Trader*'s cargo is being transferred to inland waterway craft using three floating elevators while four land-based elevators discharge it to conveyor belts which will deliver it to the silo. The photograph was taken in 1964. (*Associated British Ports*)

Opposite below: The very last vessel of the eighty registered at Wakefield between the late 1870s and 1954 was the tug/barge/ice-breaker *Alpha*, built for the A&CNC by Harkers of Knottingley in 1943. Initially, it was used on the Calder & Hebble to replace the horse towage of some of its owner's craft between Wakefield and Dewsbury, though occasionally it travelled the entire length of the Calder & Hebble. Transhipment at Wakefield, of goods formerly delivered to these premises by water, ceased. *Alpha* was transferred to Goole Docks in the 1950s and is shown, after structural alterations had been made to it, in the port's Ocean Lock in 1970.

A 2001 view of Wakefield weir and the present-day floating protection to prevent craft repeating the event shown on page 31. Former cargo-carrying craft adapted for other uses lie adjacent to Thornes Lane, including several former Hargreaves' craft (left) and the 1893-built *Brilliant Star* (described in Tempus Publishing's *The Yorkshire Ouse Navigation*) with *Neo* (mentioned in Tempus Publishing's *The Sheffield & South Yorkshire Navigation*) alongside.

Opencast coal is shown being loaded ex-lorry onto a large motor barge for carriage along the Aire & Calder in 1956. The loading staithe was built on the Thornes Lane site of the former Wakefield gasworks. *(John Goodchild Collection)*

Several maltsters were based in the Calder Valley. Edward Sutcliffe's was one of the biggest and this publicity view shows craft moored outside his large Belle Isle premises on the south bank above Wakefield flood lock. Unfortunately, newer methods of preparation tended to make the kilns obsolete and dereliction of these premises may be seen in the following photograph.

Opposite below: Belle Isle Dyeworks were established on the south bank above Wakefield flood lock in 1740. This sketch, by Henry Clarke, was made shortly before the works closed in 1890, to be replaced by a small power station which used waterborne coal to produce electricity for Wakefield's trams between 1904 and 1932. *(John Goodchild Collection)*

The Calder Carrying Co.'s towing barge *Frank W* heading upriver with the dumb vessel *Thomas Sugden* in tow during the late 1930s. *Frank W* was powered by a 40hp twin-cylinder hot bulb engine which took up so much hold space that a normal sixty ton load caused the vessel to 'have a bulk on' for'ard', making it difficult to see lock entrances, bridge holes or even to pass other craft.

J.W. Cook & Co.'s tanker barge *Dauntless*, seen here on the Humber at Hull, was a frequent visitor to Wakefield in the 1930s. The vessel brought diesel fuel from Saltend to the West Riding Bus Co.'s premises on the site of the former Belle Isle Dyeworks. Unlike other Humber waterways, the Calder & Hebble carried negligible amounts of petroleum products, mainly because its locks were too small to accommodate the tankers built from the 1920s onwards.

Most mills and factories alongside the Calder received at least an occasional barge load of coal in the nineteenth century and first half of the twentieth century. On closure, many of their wharves fell into disuse, and here *Hunt's Roger* is shown in the 1960s discharging jute from Bangladesh, imported via Hull, to a lorry near the derelict wharf and coal bunkers of the Portobello woollen mills. These formerly belonged to G&J Stubley but were being used by W.E. Rawson at the time. (*P.L. Smith*)

Approaching a bridge carrying the main Leeds-London railway line over the Calder, the waterside premises of W.E. Rawson are encountered. The photograph included in this 1930s advertisement shows the company's extensive premises to which large quantities of raw materials were imported by barge. The river flows from left to right and the railway viaduct is visible at the top of the print.

Coir was still being carried from Hull Docks to Rawsons in the 1970s but here, in March 1978 the motor barge *Bishopthorpe* has brought part of the final cargo to be delivered by water and is waiting to be discharged near the tower and chimney, both of which are visible on the company's advertisement shown previously. *(P.L. Smith)*

The Spencer Wire Co. had premises on Calder Island between Thornes Cut and the river (now a 'leisure outlet') and exported large amounts of their product by barge. A motor vessel is shown loading at the company's riverside wharf in the 1950s when three or four barges per week carried telephone wire to Hull for export to Russia.

Four
Thornes Lock to Dewsbury (Savile Town)

Hargreaves began to replace their fleet of wooden vessels delivering coal to Thornhill power station in 1970 and here the recently purchased, tiller-steered, steel motor barge *Rally* is shown above the longer of the two Thornes locks in January of that year, heading up the Calder & Hebble to join the fleet. The vessel was subsequently converted to wheel steering and fitted with a wheelhouse, instead of the weatherboard shown. Until the 1950s, the lock-keeper kept the smaller West Country size lock here ready for downstream traffic and the larger lock (122ft x 17½ ft) alongside prepared for craft coming upriver. The smaller lock fell into disuse after a change of lock-keeper. *(P.L. Smith)*

Mellors had a barge fleet and owned quarries near Elland. Most of their craft were built next to Brighouse bottom lock and used to deliver stone flags, loaded at Brookfoot or Brighouse, to Hull for export, returning to Brighouse with wheat. Until the 1930s, these vessels always sailed down to Hull and sailed back if possible, using a horse only when absolutely necessary. Mellors *Sophia*, now motorised, is seen heading past Spencers' wireworks in the 1940s loaded with coal for the higher reaches of the Calder & Hebble.

After heading out from Thornes Cut into the river, the next cut to be met is Broad Cut, dating from the 1800s. The original two canal sections hereabouts literally took short cuts across bends in the river and were slightly to the north of this present one. This 1970s view shows the present day lockhouse and bottom lock with the river flowing from the right towards the camera. A chain horse ferry crossed the river at this point until the 1950s.

Duttons' steam tug *Tybourne* which, until nationalisation, towed the company's dumb craft from the coal staithes on the Aire & Calder, where they were loaded, up the Calder & Hebble as far as Broad Cut bottom lock to be handed over to horses for onward delivery. The tug then collected empty vessels from here and took them back onto the Aire & Calder to be loaded. Duttons had the contract for supplying Thornhill power station from the 1900s until they sold out to Hargreaves who took it over in 1948.

Between the two Broad Cut locks, Hargreaves owned land on the south bank across from the towpath side where they burnt time-expired wooden vessels. The lower lock, out of shot to the right, at 120ft x 17½ ft was large enough to permit craft longer than West Country size to pass, whereas the upper lock at 65ft x 16ft was not. *Mabel*, built in 1940 as a dumb boat by Riders of Leeds and motorised in 1952, is shown being dragged from the water to be burnt in the late 1950s after a comparatively short lifetime on the Aire & Calder. *(Hargreaves)*

A light horse-drawn vessel heading down the Calder & Hebble past the lorry-fed coal staithe adjacent to Waller Bridge. The scene, between the two Broad Cut locks, appeared on a postcard published early in the twentieth century.

Ethel is shown loading coal ex-lorry at Waller Bridge staithe in the early 1960s. Larger craft working to Ferrybridge power stations could also reach this staithe but coal coming down the chute was deposited to one side of the vessel and the captain had to do much shovelling to ensure that his vessel had the desired trim. Hargreaves fitted wheelboxes to their West Country craft only after their boatmen threatened to tie up the vessels in adverse weather. *Ethel* was one of the first to be given a shelter, while Union representative Arthur Millard's *Gwendoline* was last. (*P.L. Smith*)

One of Cawoods Hargreaves push tugs is shown waiting below Broad Cut top lock as a pan is penned down in 1972 after loading above the lock. Loading on the Calder & Hebble involved crews dealing with manually operated locks and, in the case of this lock, having to work each unit through separately. About 100 tons of opencast coal was tipped into each pan, giving a draught of nearly 6ft. On the deeper Aire & Calder, they could each carry 170 tons. (*Hargreaves*)

Left: On arrival at Ferrybridge C power station, the pans are tipped after being pushed into the channel beneath the tippler as shown here.

Below: A loaded Cawoods Hargreaves pan viewed from the river as it is raised into the tippler adjacent to Ferrybridge C power station to discharge its cargo.

Above the upper Broad Cut lock lay British Oak staithe where all coal for Thornhill was loaded in the latter years of the traffic. Here, wooden barge *William Hennell* is shown passing beneath the L&YR's Bradford-Barnsley line in the 1960s as it comes to load for the power station. The barge was named after the master boatbuilder at Mirfield's Ledgard Bridge yard who retired in 1950 when the vessel was built. (*P.L. Smith*)

Hargreaves' *Ethel* swinging in Broad Cut prior to moving stern-first down to British Oak staithe to load coal for Thornhill in the 1960s. (*P.L. Smith*)

	TIME & PLACE ON BOARD	NAME OF PIT AND TIME ARRIVED	TIME AND WEIGHT LOADED	DESTINATION AND TIME ARRIVED	TIME DISCHARGED	TIME & PLACE TIED UP	FINISHING TIME	LUB OIL DRAWN	FUEL OIL DRAWN	TRAVELLING EXPENSES FROM	TO	AMOUNT	FOR OFFICE USE ONLY
MON.	11 - 0 THORNHILL	BRITISH OAK 3 - 30	5 - 20 40 - 0		2 - 0	5 - 30 BRITISH OAK	5 - 45		45 46 Double Locks	THORNES WAKEFIELD DEWSBURY BRITISH OAK WAKEFIELD	WAKEFIELD DEWSBURY THORNHILL WAKEFIELD THORNES	3d 10d 3d 8d 3d	2/3
TUES.	1 - 0 BRITISH OAK			THORNHILL 9 - 30		9 - 30 THORN-HILL	5 - 0			THORNES WAKEFIELD THORNHILL DEWSBURY WAKEFIELD	WAKEFIELD BRITISH OAK DEWSBURY WAKEFIELD THORNES	3d 9d 3d 10d 3d	2/3
WED.	11 - 0 THORNHILL	PARKHILL 12 - 30	2 - 30 16 - 0		9 - 30	4 - 30 BROAD CUT	5 - 0			THORNES WAKEFIELD DEWSBURY DURKAR LANE WAKEFIELD	WAKEFIELD DEWSBURY THORNHILL WAKEFIELD THORNES	3d 10d 3d 6d 3d	2/-
THURS.	11 - 0 BROAD CUT			THORNHILL 10 - 0		10 - 0 BR THORNHILL	5 - 0			THORNES WAKEFIELD THORNHILL DEWSBURY WAKEFIELD	WAKEFIELD DURKAR LANE DEWSBURY WAKEFIELD THORNES	3d 6d 3d 10d 3d	2/1
FRID.	11 - 0 THORNHILL	BRITISH OAK 1 - 0	2 - 30 14 - 11		11 - 0	4 - 45 DOUBLE LOCKS	5 - 0			THORNES WAKEFIELD DEWSBURY THORNHILL DEWSBURY WAKEFIELD	WAKEFIELD DEWSBURY THORNHILL DEWSBURY WAKEFIELD THORNES	3d 10d 3d 3d 10d 3d	2/-
SAT.	11 - 0 DOUBLE LOCKS			THORNHILL 8 - 0		8 - 0 THORN-HILL	12 - 0			THORNES WAKEFIELD DEWSBURY THORNHILL DEWSBURY WAKEFIELD	WAKEFIELD DEWSBURY THORNHILL DEWSBURY WAKEFIELD THORNES	3d 10d 3d 3d 10d 3d	2/8
X 113													4/-

A captain's weekly time sheet for *Ethel* dating from 1959, covering coming aboard at Thornhill on Monday morning to oversee discharge of a cargo, loading three further cargoes at British Oak and one at Parkhill on the Aire & Calder and finishing at Thornhill at midday on Saturday. Hargreaves also paid travelling expenses between the vessel and its captain's home at Thornes, near Wakefield.

Two steel motor barges are shown at British Oak staithe on a winter's day in 1978. *Integrity*, built by Harkers in 1935 along with *Rex* for Wilbys of Pontefract as dumb vessels to carry coal from Calder & Hebble staithes to York, Yorkshire's River Derwent and Thornhill, was motorised by Hargreaves after purchase in 1973. It is being loaded as *Renee*, built as a motor barge by Harkers for Hargreaves in 1946, waits.

Opposite below: Parkhill colliery was sunk in 1877 and, in common with most other collieries in the Castleford area, had part of its output allocated to Thornhill power station after the Second World War. The time sheet shown previously indicates that *Ethel* collected a cargo from here that week. Parkhill coal was also carried to gasworks at Brighouse, Elland and Sowerby Bridge. Coal bound for Ferrybridge on the Aire & Calder, however, is shown being loaded in 1979 at the 1950s-built staithe with the colliery headgear and chimney visible beyond, together with the old staithe. Both staithes were fed by rail. The colliery and staithe closed in 1983.

After loading, the cargo of coal often had to be 'trimmed' and *Elizabeth B*'s cargo is receiving this attention shortly before its voyage begins. (*P.L. Smith*)

Craft waiting to load at Hartley Bank colliery staithe in the early 1960s including *Ethelwood*, one of the 'Hull boats' which delivered to Earles' cement works alongside the River Hull. The colliery's rail link to the main line crosses the canal on the bridge beyond. The corrugated iron hut was fitted during the 1950s in an attempt to protect the loading mechanism from rusting. A similar hut was also used to cover British Oak staithe at this time. (*P.L. Smith*)

The last wooden vessel to work commercially on the Calder & Hebble was *Angela Jane*, seen here above Horbury Bridge. Unfortunately, when still at work, the barge was destroyed by fire while moored at Thornhill in February 1975. It is seen here heading up the navigation just above Horbury Bridge in the 1960s. Croxley Beck passes beneath the cut to discharge into the river beyond but, in times of flood, excess water from the beck passes into the canal through the arches visible beneath the right-hand side of the bridge.

Horbury Bridge was crossed by buses to all parts of West Yorkshire and was therefore a convenient point for captains to tie up overnight. The former Duttons' vessel *Yeponian*, coming down the Calder & Hebble to load, and a loaded barge heading up the canal are moored below the entrance to Horbury side cut (see map on page 50). (*P.L. Smith*)

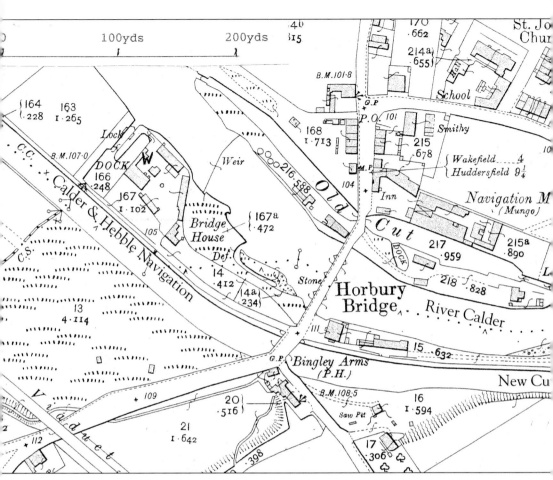

An Ordnance Survey map of the waterways at Horbury Bridge, *c*.1900. The Old Cut, north of the river, was part of the original route of the Calder & Hebble from the 1760s until 1838 when the new Broad Cut was extended along the south side of the river to join Thornhill Lees cut at Figure of Three locks. To retain access to wharves on the river and on the Old Cut, a side cut ('DOCK' on the map) and lock were built between the New Cut and the river above the weir. The C&HNC also built a warehouse here, indicated by 'W' on the map.

This view from the 1900s, looking east along the Old Cut towards the bridge at Horbury Bridge, shows a vessel that would have reached this point by using the side cut and lock to enter the river before crossing above the weir and passing through the floodgates. There was a lock at the eastern end of the Old Cut where craft could pass to rejoin the river and reach other wharves below the weir. The Old Cut was filled in during 1952.

This 2001 view of the side cut at Horbury Bridge taken from the main line of the Calder & Hebble shows the remaining upper gates of the lock into the river. The water area is now the site of residential moorings.

Formerly owned by Duttons as a dumb barge and later motorised by them, *Excelsior* is shown in 1970 leaving Millbank lock to head up the Calder & Hebble with a cargo of coal. As shown on several photographs in this book, the fitting of extension boards to a wooden vessel's coamings afforded an increase in carrying capacity.

Opposite below: Taken from a heavily-laden vessel as it approaches Double Locks, Hargreaves' steel motor barge *Fidelity*, which had a history almost identical to that of *Integrity* (see page 47), is shown heading down the navigation light in the 1970s. Savile Cut, once on the main line of the Calder & Hebble, leads off through the bridge to the right.

This much-published picture shows horse marine Emmanuel Wadsworth walking beside his animal as it hauls the wooden dumb barge *Thomas Sugden*, owned by Sugden's, the Brighouse millers. The photograph was taken near Dewsbury as the vessel passed down the Calder & Hebble between Double Locks and Millbank lock. A horse marine would be fortunate if, after being paid off by the captain of one vessel, he found another customer wanting a tow in the opposite direction shortly afterwards. Usually, he would have to tramp his horse overland back to his base using local roads.

The old main line of the Calder & Hebble fell out of use before 1800 after the enforced closure of Dewsbury Old Cut (see map on page 61). This followed arbitration over problems with water levels that construction of the original Calder & Hebble had caused for Dewsbury Mills and led to excavation of Thornhill Cut, opened in 1798, as an alternative route back into the Calder above Dewsbury. For years, the old main line lay derelict until purchased in 1878 by the A&CNC, who then built wooden warehouses in Savile Basin and worked their own craft to them. After nationalisation in 1948, BTC continued to bring craft to the premises, as shown in this photograph from the early 1950s, until they closed them in 1958. They were demolished as fire hazards in 1978.

Five
Double Locks to Shepley Bridge

The Rochdale Canal Co.'s West Country size wooden dumb boat *Beech* is shown leaving the lower lock of Double Locks while heading up the Calder & Hebble light, *c.*1920, probably after delivering a cargo loaded in Lancashire to Savile Town, Dewsbury. The company finished trading in 1921 and this vessel was bought by Duttons of Elland. One of J. Brown & Co.'s chemical works is just visible in the background. The Rochdale Canal Co. had several keels built at Calder & Hebble boatyards. *Beech* was one of these, launched at Battyeford in 1914 and No.313 of 373 vessels built and registered in Mirfield.

Hargreaves' *No.61*, bound for Thornhill power station with a cargo of coal, is photographed in 1979 between the two Double Locks.

A horse-drawn A&CNC flyboat leaving the upper lock of Double Locks while heading down the Calder & Hebble from either Brighouse or Huddersfield in the early 1900s.

In 1905, the Midland Railway made an unsuccessful attempt to avoid Leeds and reach Bradford from Royston, near Barnsley, via Dewsbury. This entailed crossing the Calder & Hebble above Double Locks by the viaduct shown here under construction.

Further up the cut, Thornhill Iron & Steel Co. had premises and a wharf on the left-hand side, shown in this photograph on a postcard sent in 1900. An explosion here in 1914 led to closure of the premises.

In 1927, James Austin & Sons bought the Thornhill site and re-established the iron and steel business. A barge is visible at their wharf discharging into the works in the 1930s.

A power station was built at Thornhill in the early 1900s and this postcard shows it standing in isolation at this time on the south bank of the river above Long Cut end.

Opposite below: As demand for electricity rose the power station was extended and a riverside wharf fitted with rail-mounted grabs was built, as shown in this photograph taken in the 1930s from the Ravensthorpe bank. Fifty to sixty 75 ton cargoes were delivered there each week at this time and, in the 1940s and 1950s, it was usual to see as many as twenty loaded craft waiting to be discharged.

From 1904, coal was delivered from numerous colliery staithes on both the Calder & Hebble and Aire & Calder to Thornhill power station in vessels owned by Duttons of Elland. A cargo may be seen being discharged from barge to horse and cart prior to admission into the works in the days when demand for electricity was small.

Coal discharge facilities at Thornhill power station were moved from the river to the still waters of Long Cut in 1953. The Calder Carrying Co.'s wooden vessels *Cooper Bridge* and *Wakefield* are here taking part in the opening ceremony at the new wharf. (*Hargreaves*)

Right: Taken in 1979 when all coal brought to Thornhill power station was loaded at British Oak staithe and all eight vessels on the five-mile, five-lock voyage were built of steel, this photograph shows part of the fleet at the power station. *Haddlesey* (furthest from the camera) delivered the final load of 70.42 tonnes (69.30 tons) here on Friday 31 July 1981, bringing regular commercial traffic on the Calder & Hebble to an end. A modern gas-fired power station has since been built on the site.

Below: The navigation at the junction of Long Cut and the river was quite close to the original wharves for Dewsbury, dating from 1762, The Calder & Hebble had to be rerouted in 1798, as described on page 54, leaving the situation as shown on this sketch map. Note the 200 yard long Fearnley's Cut, opened in 1835, which was almost parallel with Dewsbury Old Cut, joined the river at 'A'.

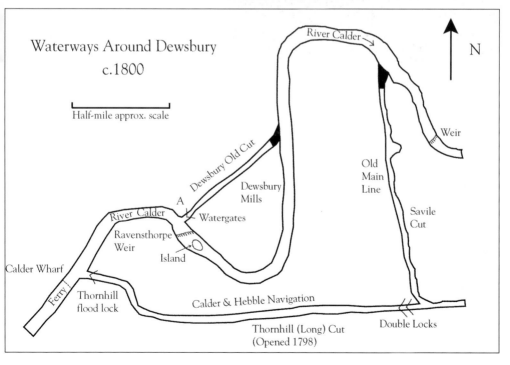

Waterways Around Dewsbury
c.1800

Half-mile approx. scale

River Calder

N

Weir

Dewsbury Old Cut

Dewsbury Mills

Old Main Line

A

River Calder

Watergates

Savile Cut

Ravensthorpe Weir

Island

Calder Wharf

Ferry

Thornhill flood lock

Calder & Hebble Navigation

Double Locks

Thornhill (Long) Cut
(Opened 1798)

Wharves on Dewsbury Old Cut still functioned until well after 1798 and these were reached by using the river below Long Cut end. This was also the route to Fearnley's Cut and this postcard view shows one of the two arches of the 1847-built L&NWR bridge over the route downriver, near which there were rowing boats for hire in the 1900s.

Many cargoes of imported myrabolams, acorn-like nuts from India used by tanners to make leather more pliable, were discharged at the wharves on Fearnley's Cut. Here sacks of these items are being transhipped from ship to barge in Goole Docks for delivery to the Calder & Hebble.

Above Ravensthorpe weir, Dewsbury Old Cut used to lead off via flood gates to by-pass a section of the river before rejoining it at a lock at the other end of the cut. The river and weir are just visible beneath the footbridge, over the watergates, in this view of the western end of the Old Cut. The pipe bridge or 'aqueduct' shown on this card may also be seen on the upper illustration opposite. The Old Cut is dry and much wider nowadays in its function as a flood relief channel, with the part shown here almost totally covered by concrete.

Heading up the Calder and looking back downriver after passing Long Cut end, this view of the woollen mills of Ravensthorpe could once be seen. All the mills received occasional cargoes of coal by barge to fuel their boilers. None of the chimneys remain, though some of the mill walls have been retained on the riverbank, providing extra security for the premises.

This downriver view at Ravensthorpe shows moored barges on the northern bank as a vessel crosses the river to enter Long Cut, close to the power station. The road bridge was opened in the late nineteenth century and was then usually used by boathorses to cross the river instead of the horse ferry at the cut end. (Shown on page 12).

Greenwood Cut flood gates (see page 10) lie just off the right of this view of *Marjorie R*, a steel motor barge built by Harkers for Hargreaves in 1946 along with a si0ster vessel, *Renee*. The photograph was taken in 1985 on the river section between Greenwood cut and Mirfield cut after regular cargo-carrying on the Calder & Hebble had finished. Three of the craft formerly used on the British Oak-Thornhill traffic were used to remove spoil excavated as a new sewer was under construction by Yorkshire Water Authority.

Six
Mirfield &
Battyeford Cuts

A postcard view of a light vessel approaching Shepley Bridge lock at the eastern end of the 1776-built Mirfield cut as the gate on the towpath side is being opened. The picture, dating from the 1900s, appears to have been set up for the photographer as there are no signs of a horse or other means of propulsion of the barge. (*Miss C. Humpleby Collection*)

Single-storey lock-keepers' cottages were once an attractive feature of the Calder & Hebble. Several have now been demolished, but this one at Shepley Bridge, situated above the junction between the river and Mirfield cut and visible on the previous photograph, is still standing. The drydock to the left, shown on this postcard from the 1910s, also remains in use.

Shepley Bridge boatyard was established in 1776 and is visible to the right of the vessel in the picture on page 65. The yard was owned by Albert Wood, a canal carrier of Sowerby Bridge, from 1900. Preparations are shown being made in 1910 for the launch of his West Country keel *Eddie*, the final vessel to be built here. The size of the vessel allowed it to trade anywhere on the Calder & Hebble route between Liverpool and Hull.

After the launch of *Eddie*, Shepley Bridge yard was used for the maintenance of Albert Wood's fleet until he gave up carrying in 1924, thirty years after he began. This picture comes from the photograph album kept by his late son and features carpenters at the yard standing aboard *Sam* in 1911.

As on many waterways, redundant commercial craft are often converted for leisure use and *Integrity*, (see page 47) moored outside Mirfield's Navigation Inn in 2001, regularly cruises on the Calder & Hebble.

TELEGRAMS·
"CROWTHER
MIRFIELD."
TELEPHONE·
MIRFIELD 44.

EAST THORPE MALT HOUSES.

J. F. & J. CROWTHER LTD.,

MALTSTERS.

MAKERS OF PATENT CRYSTALLIZED
OAK DRIED AND ROASTED MALTS.

MIRFIELD. YORKSHIRE.

At one time, sixteen maltsters were based in Mirfield, all receiving grain by water. One of these, J.F. & J. Crowther, was established in the late eighteenth century. The company subsequently acquired premises across the canal from their original site and built a high-level bridge across the waterway, featured on this company letterhead dating from the 1900s. The inset etchings show some of the company's other maltings. By the late 1920s, they had eight canalside plants in the town.

A photograph from the 1930s showing a vessel in the early stages of construction at Ledgard Bridge yard, Mirfield, adjacent to Crowthers. The yard was established in 1790 and hundreds of West Country size craft were built here. *BraDsyldA* (see page 79) was the last vessel of 373 to be registered at Mirfield under the Canal Boats Act on 27 January 1954. As at all boatyards on the Calder & Hebble, craft were built entirely of wood, though composite craft with iron knees and frames to support wooden planks were being built elsewhere from the turn of the century.

A recently launched vessel built at Ledgard Bridge yard is shown in the side arm of the canal
with the launch party standing aboard on this photograph dating from the 1920s. Almost all
the Calder Carrying Co.'s fleet were built at this yard.

A few feet away from the bows of the vessel in the previous illustration lay
the boatyard's dry dock and Duttons' recently motorised dumb barge *Regal*
is shown after the fitting of almost a complete new bow section in the
1940s. Craft were usually built of English oak with an elm bottom.

Wooden West Country vessels built since 1940 at Ledgard Bridge Boatyard, Mirfield

Launched	Name
1943	*Sowerby Bridge*
1945	*Brookfoot*
1948	*No 48*
1949	*Angela Jane*
1950	*William Hennell*
1951	*Elizabeth B*
1952	*Ethel*
1953	*Gwendoline*
1954	*BraDsyldA*
1955	*Isobel*

Notes

1, *BraDsyldA* was built for the Bradford Dyers Association. All other craft were constructed for the Calder Carrying Company which became a Hargreaves subsidiary after Nationalisation in 1948.

2, The yard remained open until December 1973 for the repair of craft.

Hargreaves' *Gwendoline* before launching at Ledgard Bridge yard in August 1953 with holidaying schoolboys waiting to view the event. *(Hargreaves)*

The launch in 1955 of *Isobel*, probably the last new wooden barge to be built for commercial carrying on a British waterway. The vessel was fitted with a 21hp Lister diesel engine. *(Hargreaves)*

Traditionally, owners, boat builders and the future captain accompanied a new vessel on its trial run. *Sowerby Bridge* is shown setting out from Mirfield on such a trip in April 1943, shortly to pass out of the western end of the cut and into the river.

As well as building new boats, craft were repaired at Ledgard Bridge yard. Engines were fitted to dumb craft, especially in the 1930s and 1940s and here, Clegg Brothers' *George* is moored on the towpath side of the canal within sight of St Paul's distinctive church tower in October 1943, waiting to be fitted with a National diesel engine.

Floodgates at the western end of Mirfield cut had been converted to a flood lock in 1883, enabling vessels then to pass at most high river levels. This illustration looks back at Ledgard Bridge yard from the flood lock above in the 1920s with Crowthers' premises close to the boatyard. At the time of this photograph, only two maltsters remained in Mirfield: Sutcliffes, which closed in 1956; and Crowthers, which survived until taken over and closed in 1972.

A photograph taken in the 1930s from the towpath bridge over the river above Mirfield as Clegg Brothers' *Cresol*, formerly owned by L.B. Holliday & Co., is hauled by horse up the Calder & Hebble with a cargo of coal for Sowerby Bridge gasworks.

An aerial view of the navigation at Mirfield from the 1930s, showing the towpath bridge across the river and the weir and flood lock at the top of Mirfield cut. (The towpath bridge was demolished about 1958 leaving only the central pier shown on page 11). Butt End Mill, at the lower left of the picture, dates from 1804 and was notorious for illegally drawing off excessive volumes of water, via the goits shown, to power its machinery, thereby lowering the level in this reach of the river and in Mirfield cut by up to 2ft, grounding several craft for at least a day. A deputation of angry boatmen stranded by this act once visited the mill and the confrontation led to the police becoming involved. A similar situation, though not as severe, existed at Ravensthorpe and some other mill sites on the navigation. (*Frances Stott Collection*)

Opposite top: Looking downriver to the towpath 'turnover' bridge and Kilners' Fold Head mill where woollen yarns were spun, this photograph from the 1920s also shows the distant Mirfield flood lock in the centre, from which the river flows off right to head over the weir. (*Miss C. Humpleby Collection*)

Moving upriver from Mirfield, the next cut to be met is the one at Battyeford where another boatyard had been established. Hollidays' *Cresol*, dating from 1916, was amongst the many vessels built here. A vessel is seen heading up the navigation past the yard with the entrance lock and lock cottage just visible beyond. It was while *Cresol* was being built that the Cleggs met Mr Holliday's foreman who persuaded them to work for him, initially on *Phenol* (see page 66, when this vessel was named *Eddie*), and subsequently on *Cresol*. Between 1916 and 1930, the Cleggs worked these horse boats across the Pennines via the Rochdale Canal, Bridgewater Canal and River Mersey to collect nitric and sulphuric acids from the chemical works at Runcorn – a two-week round trip. Occasionally, they would also travel to Browns, near Double Locks at Dewsbury, to load carboys of hydrochloric acid. Hollidays were situated alongside the Huddersfield Broad Canal and, initially, used these substances in the manufacture of explosives for the war effort, later branching out into the production of synthetic dyes.

Looking north-east towards Battyeford, a vessel may be seen nearing completion on the 'island' between canal cut and river. The South Pennine Boat Club took over this boatyard site in 1985 and excavated moorings for its members' craft. (*Miss C. Humpleby Collection*)

Looking down the navigation towards Battyeford boatyard (beyond the bridge) in the 1910s, the navigation maintenance gang have been posed, together with their fleet. The front outer vessel has been cut down amidships for ease of wheeling plant on and off. (*Miss C. Humpleby Collection*)

Seven

Battyeford to Huddersfield

Turning right at the top end of Battyeford cut and following the river down towards the weir, this scene would probably have been encountered in the early 1900s with craft discharging or waiting to discharge grain or coal at Stott's flour mill adjacent to the weir. A 'Yorkshire Narrowboat' with approximate dimensions of 55ft x 7ft and therefore able to use all the waterways of the region, lies tied up in the foreground. Full-length narrowboats (70ft x 7ft) were too long to pass through Calder & Hebble locks, while craft of West Country size were too wide to use the Huddersfield Narrow Canal.

On 15 April 1909, Stott's four-storey flour mill, leased from the C&HNC, was destroyed by a fire which broke out on the second floor. The event was commemorated on a series of postcards from which this picture was selected.

Turning left at the top end of Battyeford cut to follow the river upstream, after crossing the horse bridge shown on page 11, this late nineteenth century view of the bridge just used by the horse hauling the loaded vessel shown was obtained from beneath the 1900-built L&NWR bridge carrying the Huddersfield-Leeds line. Despite the horse, a caption to this postcard view saw smoke from the vessel's cabin fire as evidence that the barge was 'in steam'!

Within a short distance of the previous view, Cooper Bridge lock and cut are met and here, Bradford Dyers'Association's *BraDsyldA*, captained by Arthur Clegg (left), has penned down the lock while heading east for another load of coal with engine room door open and boathooks at the ready. On motor boats, the smallest hook was always filed sharp for cutting away any plastic sheeting or other obstacles which fouled the propeller.

This lock lobby was provided for the Cooper Bridge lock-keeper's use during working hours. In the 1920s, however, the lock-keeper actually slept here, there being insufficient room for him as well as his large family in the nearby lock cottage. Horse marines occasionally slept here too when away from base, though they usually bedded down on the cabin floor of the boat that they were hauling. The structure is still standing and is used by BW as a store.

The Calder Carrying Co.'s wooden motor vessel *Sowerby Bridge* is seen heading light down Cooper Bridge cut towards the lock on a winter day in the 1940s. During the Second World War, the vessel carried coal to Earles' cement factory up the Harbour at Hull and returned with sacks of grain or cocoa beans loaded in the city's docks, the latter cargo for storage alongside the Calder & Hebble. Here, with iron sheathing above and below the waterline to prevent ice penetrating its wooden hull, it is on ice-breaking duties between Brighouse and Ravensthorpe. (*Douglas Carey*)

Above: Taken from Cooper Bridge in 1951, Sugdens' *David Sugden* is shown chasing *Thomas Sugden* down Cooper Bridge cut towards the lock. The former vessel was a purpose-built motor towing barge while the latter was a former dumb craft, motorised in the 1940s. Both vessels have hatches and covers in place, indicating that they are probably heading for Hull to collect sixty-plus ton cargoes of grain for their owners' Brighouse mill.

Opposite bottom: This view taken looking up the cut towards the floodgates from beneath Cooper Bridge in the early 1950s shows coal-laden craft, including the Calder Carrying Co.'s *Frank W* (right) and *Marie* (left), held up by ice outside the former C&HNC warehouse while en route to Huddersfield power station. The steps were for the use of boat captains who had to hand in their toll notes to the C&HNC official based here. *(Ken Kettle)*

Cooper Bridge weir was damaged by floods in 1939 and the C&HNC begged *Mary*, an old vessel, to try to stem the breach as shown. Before the leak was sealed and the waterway kept open for traffic however, the navigation company had to buy and beg bales of shoddy (ground up woollen material, to be recycled after blending with new wool) from a nearby mill to put around the barge. *(Ken Kettle)*

Repair of the breach shown in the previous illustration was eventually effected by hiring a pile driver to construct a dam around *Mary*, allowing workmen to rebuild the top of the weir. *(Ken Kettle)*

This 1920s downriver view from Cooper Bridge shows the weir (left) and the footbridge over the entrance to the first lock of the Huddersfield Broad Canal. Prior to the Second World War, this waterway was the exclusive preserve of horse boats.

An aerial view dating from the 1950s also showing the Huddersfield Broad Canal (to the left) but mainly featuring the L.B. Holliday chemical complex at Deighton, about one mile up from Cooper Bridge. Major Holliday was recalled from active service in the First World War to set up an explosives factory on this formerly greenfield site and the sloop-rigged *Leticia* was built to transport these by sea to Woolwich Arsenal via the Thames. Between 1916 and 1930, the company operated a fleet of horse-drawn vessels on the Calder & Hebble and adjoining waterways. (See page 75).

After purchase of the Huddersfield Broad Canal by the C&HNC and subsequent nationalisation, the waterway experienced an upsurge in traffic as Hargreaves signed a six-year contract in 1947 to supply coal to Huddersfield power station. Years of decline had affected the canal however, and initially seventy-five-ton capacity vessels were delivering only thirty-five tons due to its shallow channel. There also seemed to be problems at every one of its nine locks. Eventually, loads of around sixty tons were being carried. Here *Elland*, returning light from Huddersfield, found difficulty in passing beneath the bridge adjacent to one of the mid-flight locks. An anchor, moved from stern to bow of the vessel, eventually solved the problem. (*Douglas Carey*)

BEIGHTON
RED DOLE LOCK

About one mile out of Huddersfield, having just penned down the canal's top lock, this laden horse boat is rounding the bend at Canker Lane while heading towards Cooper Bridge. A canal maintenance vessel is moored on the bend as a long goods train climbs up the L&NWR line to the left. The illustration appeared on a postcard used in 1911.

Opposite below: A general view of the site of the Huddersfield Broad Canal's Red Doles lock featured on the previous picture. (*Trevor Ellis Collection*)

Looking south towards Huddersfield town centre as Gasworks Bridge takes Leeds Road and its tramlines across the canal, this aerial view from the 1930s shows a barge and its horse after discharge onto the wharfside of the vessel's cargo of builders' lime.

A vessel loaded with a low density cargo lies moored below the Huddersfield Broad Canal's Turnbridge facing down the navigation in the 1910s. (*Trevor Ellis Collection*)

The Huddersfield Broad Canal's most famous feature is the Turnbridge or Locomotive Bridge, built in 1865 to replace a conventional swing bridge. Two chains fastened to the bridge platform each pass over two wheels to connect with a large counterweight, as shown, allowing the structure to be lifted vertically and opened for canal traffic by the efforts of one individual. The adjacent footbridge beyond, which is not visible on the previous picture, was provided in the twentieth century to minimise delays to pedestrians.

About 100yds above the Turnbridge, close to the town centre, lay the wharf of timber merchants Jarratt, Pyrah & Armitage, shown on this 1940s advertising card. Carrying such a low-density material as wood, the craft shown have their cargoes stacked high, making it difficult for the helmsman too see over the 'bulk'. Navigational practice was to dash to each side of the vessel in turn to see ahead when entering a lock or approaching a narrow bridgehole. A supermarket now occupies the timber merchants' former waterside site.

Timber was usually imported via Hull or Goole and trans-shipped to inland waterway craft for transport to inland wharves such as that shown at Huddersfield in the previous illustration. Here River Benue is shown transferring such a cargo in Hull docks. (*Associated British Ports*)

Aire & Calder dumb craft moored outside their 1865-built wooden extensions to the original 1778-built warehouse, adjacent to and above Wakefield Road bridge in Huddersfield. Cargoes to and from full-length (70ft) narrowboats able to use the Huddersfield Narrow Canal but not the Broad Canal were transhipped here for onward carriage by water. The photograph was taken in the 1920s looking towards the Huddersfield Broad Canal. The hand-crane on a cast iron base with its wooden jib and stone counterbalance has been preserved, while the warehouse itself has been converted into apartments.

Opposite below: Having a much shorter life than its sister vessel *No.61*, Hargreaves first West Country size steel motor vessel, *No.60*, built by Harkers in 1938, is shown in this view looking south-east. The barge is moored just below Aspley Basin preparing to discharge coal for lorrying to the power station at Huddersfield in 1947. The vessel was scrapped in 1957. New coal hoppers were built in the basin to receive power station coal in 1949. The contract ended in 1953 and there has been no further regular commercial traffic to Huddesfield since then.

Though reopened for leisure use in 2001, commercial cross-Pennine traffic on the Huddersfield Narrow Canal had almost ceased by 1910, but coal was delivered on the length above Huddersfield as far as Marsden for several more years. Here the light horse-drawn Yorkshire Narrowboat *Reliance* is shown, in the 1900s, descending one of the forty-two locks between Marsden and Huddersfield, probably to collect a cargo of coal from Calder & Hebble collieries. (*David L. Finnis Collection*)

A loaded horse-drawn full length narrowboat is shown in lock 21W at Uppermill, heading east in the 1900s. If bound for Huddersfield, the vessel would continue rising to lock 32W, negotiate Standedge Tunnel and then fall through the forty-two locks on the eastern side of the Huddersfield Narrow Canal. (*Trevor Ellis Collection*)

Eight
Brighouse, Brookfoot & Elland

Between Cooper Bridge and Brighouse, the Calder & Hebble leaves the Calder for another canal cut at Kirklees bottom lock. This postcard view showing the cut and lock at its lower end was taken in the 1930s looking upstream from Wakefield Road on the opposite bank of the river. About 200yds above Kirklees top lock there was a fresh water spring which ensured that horses increased their towing speed as they approached it.

Dating from around 1900 when whole families lived aboard trading vessels, this horse-drawn vessel appears to have fires in both fore and aft cabins as it heads up the river section near Brighouse.

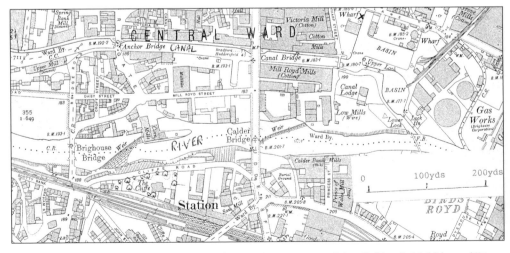

This illustration comprises part of an Ordnance Survey map of the Calder & Hebble and River Calder at Brighouse dating from the 1900s. The first eighteenth century canal cut was made merely to by-pass the two mill weirs on the river. It was extended in 1780 to meet the river further upstream and subsequently extended even further to Brookfoot.

The towpath bridge shown on this photograph of the bottom lock at Brighouse, taken from across the Calder, was swept away by floods in the 1940s and never replaced. From 1815, the Calder & Hebble was all canal from here up to Halifax and Sowerby Bridge.

The Brighouse millers Thomas Sugden & Son were established in 1829. This upriver view from Calder Bridge shows the town's upper weir and Old Brighouse Mill which the company had acquired at the time of this postcard view dating from the 1900s. This was subsequently rebuilt and enlarged and another mill nearby was purchased, thus giving Sugden's property that extended from the river to the canal, over 100yds away.

A white horse in the distance is shown hauling a loaded vessel out of Brighouse bottom lock into the lower basin in this 1920s view. Coal for the gasworks was discharged to the right and craft are visible in the upper basin, reached by passage up another lock. Coal ceased to be delivered to these gasworks, as well as those at Elland and Sowerby Bridge, in the early 1950s.

Opposite below: After being horse-hauled to Wakefield, the flyboat in the previous photograph would make its way to Goole by using the Aire & Calder's steam towage service between Fall Ings lock and Goole, having moored in the position shown on page 20. One such tow is seen heading beneath the Great North Road bridge while coming down the River Aire at Ferrybridge in the 1920s.

A light Aire & Calder flyboat heads into Brighouse top lock in the 1920s with the gasworks again visible. The vessel would probably have discharged its cargo at the C&HNC's warehouse in the upper basin and be on its way back to Goole or Hull.

Goole. — Tide Time.

Above: Should the A&C Flyboat be bound for Hull, further east than Goole, another tow, this time by one of the Goole & Hull Steam Towing Co.'s tugs, would be necessary. This late nineteenth century photograph shows a tug with a line of barges in tow preparing to leave Goole and head down the Ouse. A sea-going sailing barge and a steamship are also visible while, in the foreground, barges loaded with timber wait to enter the docks after coming upriver.

Left: Back at Brighouse in 1975 and restored by volunteers, *Ethel* is being turned in the entrance to Brighouse upper basin with the top lock visible to the right. The late Peter Smith, a man with boundless enthusiasm for the Calder & Hebble and its commercial traffic, is standing at the stern of the vessel with shaft at the ready. Shortly afterwards, the vessel was taken over the Pennines via the Leeds & Liverpool Canal to be displayed at Ellesmere Port Boat Museum. Ten years later, it was in an advanced state of decay and could not be kept afloat.

A vessel discharging cargo in the early 1930s onto the raised platform at Brighouse wire wharf, with the adjacent C&HNC warehouse (located by X on the O.S. map on page 92) visible to the left. Local factories collected their requirements from here, the platform making it easier to load the coils of wire onto their lorries and carts.

A 'go anywhere' Yorkshire Narrowboat (see pages 77 and 90) discharging sand collected from the riverbed near Brookfoot at Brighouse on the side arm just west of Canal Bridge, using the labour-intensive shovel, barrow and plank method.

THEIR MANUFACTURES STILL STAND SECOND TO NONE

Unloading Grain at our Brighouse Flour Mills

Thos. SUGDEN & Son Ltd.

CORN MILLERS

BRIGHOUSE

ESTABLISHED 1829

Left: An advertisement dating from the 1930s for the Brighouse millers and barge owners. The picture, looking back down the canal from Anchor Bridge, shows their wooden dumb craft *Thomas Sugden* and *Richard Sugden* discharging grain brought from Hull at their canalside mill. The barge fleet was disbanded in the 1960s, though grain supplies were then delivered to Wakefield, and subsequently Stanley Ferry, for onward carriage by lorry.

Below: A light wooden vessel being manoeuvred into Ganny Lock above Brighouse in the 1920s while coming down the Calder & Hebble, as the mate or horse marine holds the coiled horse line.

BRIGHOUSE GANNY LOCK, ON THE CANAL NEAR BROOKFOOT.

Both river and canal take a ninety degree turn at Brookfoot, which is evident from this 1910s view. The Red Beck, flowing in from the left at the most acute point of the bend, provides water for the canal before passing through a sluice into the Calder. It also deposits silt, leaving this stretch of canal in need of almost constant dredging. The canal is drained in this photograph and a maintenance boat is sitting on the bed, indicating that repair work to the canal is underway. (*Trevor Ellis Collection*)

The Bradford Dyers' Association was established in 1898 when several firms involved in the dyeing of wool and its blends with other fibres, joined together. The company generated its own steam and electricity at Brookfoot using waterborne coal. The BDA's steel motor vessel *Draepwelle*, built by Harkers in 1949 and fitted with a Widdop engine but no ballast tanks, is shown moored at the company's canalside coal storage bunker on land between the Calder & Hebble and Red Beck. In addition to this vessel, the company also owned the wooden *BraDsyldA*, built using kiln-dried timber in 1954 (see page 79) and often compared favourably with its steel sister vessel as it had a ballast tank on either side of the fuel tank making it more stable when light. The company also received cargoes of coal from other carriers until they ended waterway involvement in 1958.

This postcard view, taken from the eastern end of the flat Calder Valley bottom between Elland and Brighouse, shows the river and canal with the straight 1808-built Freeman's cut stretching away towards Elland from Brookfoot lock in the middle distance. Huge quantities of stone from quarries at Cromwell Bottom and Southowram, north of the canal, were loaded into craft shown moored at wharves on the right of the picture. Initially the stone was delivered to the wharfside by horse and cart. This 'Yorkshire Stone' was used in the foundations of Blackpool Tower, during repairs to the Tower of London and in the widening of London Bridge. Large quantities were also exported to Germany and used in construction of many of Hamburg's streets and buildings. Brookfoot mill is prominent near the lock. Originally a cotton mill, becoming disused before purchase by confectionery manufacturers in 1908 and subsequently by carpet makers in 1939, it is now a retail outlet.

A present day view of the Calder & Hebble below Brookfoot lock with the main line passing beneath the bridge. The heavily overgrown floodgates to the left, dating from the late eighteenth century, allowed craft to pass between the river and canal section before Freeman's Cut was made.

The floodgates shown in the previous picture were kept in use until the mid-twentieth century to allow craft access to the river and riverside sand and gravel pits beyond. The Brighouse sand boat shown on page 97 is seen at work in the 1900s dredging sand by using the poles and ropes shown, to drag a leather bag with an iron-rimmed mouth along the river bed. On occasions, the vessel also dredged silt brought into the canal at Brookfoot by Red Beck. (*Trevor Ellis Collection*)

Although a cut at Tag Hole featured on Smeaton's original mid-eighteenth century map, Tag lock and lockhouse were not built until 1808 at the eastern end of a cut to by-pass a stretch of river between Brighouse and Elland. Said to be named after a local ghost, it was never part of the main Calder & Hebble because Freeman's Cut was built at the same time, though a sand and gravel pit was developed on the 'island' between river and cut and craft came here to load. The cut became an attractive pleasure boating and strolling area for local residents in the early twentieth century, as shown on this postcard illustration. A nature reserve was subsequently established and an angling club introduced fish stocks, but the area has since also proved attractive as a landfill site for waste and its original characteristics have been almost obliterated.

Looking down the navigation from Crowther Bridge between Brighouse and Elland, the Calder Carrying Co.'s *Frank W* is attempting to free a loaded vessel from the ice of early 1948. When ice formed on the Calder & Hebble, *Frank W* was responsible for the Elland-Brighouse length with *Sowerby Bridge* allocated to the Brighouse-Raventhorpe stretch.

A horse-drawn vessel is shown emerging from Crowther Bridge, a stone-built structure with brick parapet, en route for Elland in the mid-1900s.

With the lady of the boat seated peeling potatoes and a fire in both the aft cabin and the lock
hut, a boat captain holds *Cyril Bedford*'s iron tiller hard over to counter the water coming down
the byewash as his heavily laden vessel runs into Park Nook lock, near Elland, in the 1920s.
The towing horse is standing on the lockside as the lock-keeper leans on one of his lower gates.
The photograph was taken by local photographer Albert Townsend. *(Peter Spence Collection)*

Left: Coal traffic to gasworks at Brighouse, Elland and Sowerby Bridge was an important feature of the Calder & Hebble during the first half of the twentieth century. Here, a vessel is being discharged at Elland gasworks in 1915 before installation of a more modern hoist to unload cargoes.

Below: Some of the coal for Calder & Hebble gasworks came from the Barnsley Canal, which leaves the River Calder about a mile below Fall Ings lock at Wakefield and rises through fifteen locks. A light vessel is shown here, at Agbrigg, heading between the second and third locks in the flight bound for one of the waterway's colliery staithes to load.

This scene was photographed looking down the Calder & Hebble from Elland's Halifax Road Bridge, with coal-laden craft belonging to the locally based canal carrying company, established by William Dutton in the 1830s, moored at the town wharf. The output of a cooper and cask maker may be seen on the wharfside ready to be loaded onto craft. A barge is also tied up outside the door of the covered wet dock within the warehouse and a vessel lies beneath the gasworks gantry beyond. Duttons' crews continued to live aboard their vessels until nationalisation in 1948. (*Peter Spence Collection*)

Above: A day out on a swept-out barge was a common event for many groups in the early twentieth century. Staging was fitted into the vessel's hold and here, in 1911, the horse-drawn *Edward* is preparing to leave from outside the covered wet dock at Elland for Shepley Bridge with a party from the Salvation Army.

Left: After Hollidays ceased to carry their chemicals by barge in 1930, former employees, the Clegg Brothers, purchased their own four-strong fleet and took over the Sowerby Bridge gasworks' coal contract. Here, in the 1930s, their *William* pens through Woodside Mill lock above Elland with a load of coal while their horse waits, feeding from a bucket.

This northwards-looking view of the canal and river from Hullen Edge shows Woodside Mill lock to the right, but is dominated by the mill itself with smoke issuing from the chimney. A vessel is visible discharging beneath one of the canopies and three craft are waiting above the mill. *(Peter Spence Collection)*

Looking back towards the lock, a long queue of loaded craft may be seen waiting to discharge at Elland's Woodside Mills in 1907. The mills were owned by Leethams of York at this time and, in addition to cargoes of coal and grain, several craft were carrying ready-milled flour. *(Ron Gosney Collection)*

This postcard view shows another view of a queue outside Woodside Mills, dating from the same time as the previous photograph but looking up the Calder & Hebble rather than down it. A similar situation existed during the Second World War as craft loaded with cocoa beans from a shipload, often of over 10,000 tons, brought them onto the Calder & Hebble for storage. Canal company warehouses at Horbury Bridge, Brighouse and Elland were used for the purpose, in addition to the many mills made idle by shortage of manpower. Coincidentally, this cargo also had links with York because the beans were eventually returned to Wakefield or Goole for delivery to Rowntrees of York, the chocolate manufacturers, in craft owned by T.F. Wood & Co. *(Ron Gosney Collection)*

Visible on both preceding photographs is the lobby provided by Leethams for boat people from the waiting craft. A central fireplace with an oven on each side and copper boilers in each corner of the room provided baking and washing facilities.

110

Nine
Salterhebble to Halifax & Sowerby Bridge

Canal and road follow a parallel path from Elland in the distance to reach the bottom one of the three Salterhebble locks where the road from Greetland to Halifax (Staniland Road) crosses the picture diagonally, bridging the canal at Brooksmouth. The confluence of Hebble Brook, flowing down from Halifax on a course parallel to this road, and the River Calder may be seen to the right of the view.

A loaded vessel coming up the navigation passes beneath Staniland Road bridge as it approaches the bottom gates of Brooksmouth lock in the 1920s.

Left: The guillotine bottom gate shown was fitted to Brooksmouth lock in 1938 when widening of the Greetland-Halifax road bridge brought it too close to the lock and made the ordinary bottom gates unworkable. A pleasure craft is shown leaving the lock in 2001 after the gate has been raised electrically. Visually, this area is very attractive but several sewage works in the vicinity detract from its appeal.

Opposite below: Originally, to complete the change in level of the waterway, a staircase pair of locks (where an intermediate gate acted as top gate to the lower lock and bottom gate to the upper lock) were built here. This proved unsatisfactory and was replaced by two conventional locks in 1780. The lock cottage shown lies adjacent to the upper of these two locks. The bridge behind it carries the 1844-opened Halifax branch railway link to the Manchester-Leeds main line over the Salterhebble-Sowerby Bridge summit level of the Calder & Hebble.

With Stanley Ferry aqueduct on the Aire & Calder, Standedge tunnel on the Huddersfield Narrow Canal and the spectacular scenery, tunnels, aqueducts and bridges of the Rochdale Canal, the Calder & Hebble may seem to lack its share of distinctive waterway 'features'. It has no tunnels and now the only aqueduct is this one taking the waterway over Hebble Brook just above Brooksmouth lock a short distance from the brook's confluence with the River Calder. There was another aqueduct over Hebble Brook on the Halifax Branch.

Lock House. Salterhebble. Halifax.

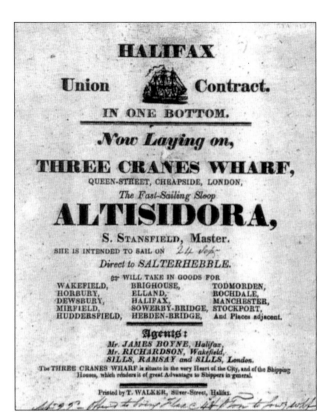

Left: Turning right after penning up the top lock at Salterhebble, a basin is encountered where goods for Halifax were originally discharged before construction of the Halifax Branch. This 1820s advertisement for the London to Salterhebble 'fast sailing sloop' *Altisidora* dates from this time. The vessel would voyage from the Thames via the East Coast, Rivers Humber and Ouse, the Aire & Calder from Goole to Wakefield and, finally, the Calder & Hebble.

Below: A boatyard was established in Salterhebble basin and this westward-looking postcard view of the canal shows both basin and boatyard. The Hebble Brook may be glimpsed through the trees to the left.

Notes on the text accompanying the above picture, published in a local newspaper of July 1936.

For over a century and a half, Halifax has had its own dry dock at Salterhebble, and it is still in use. Boats enter the dock through lock gates which are then closed, and the water is drained out by gravitation through a sluice into the Hebble Brook. No pumping is required. The dock is chiefly used for repair of the Calder and Hebble Navigation Co.'s boats and the sixty-year-old boat illustrated is used to carry materials for repairs to the canals and works. The timbers are of English oak and there are about twenty tons of wood used in its construction. Building and repair is an expensive operation, particularly so since the boatbuilder still plies his craft almost entirely by hand.

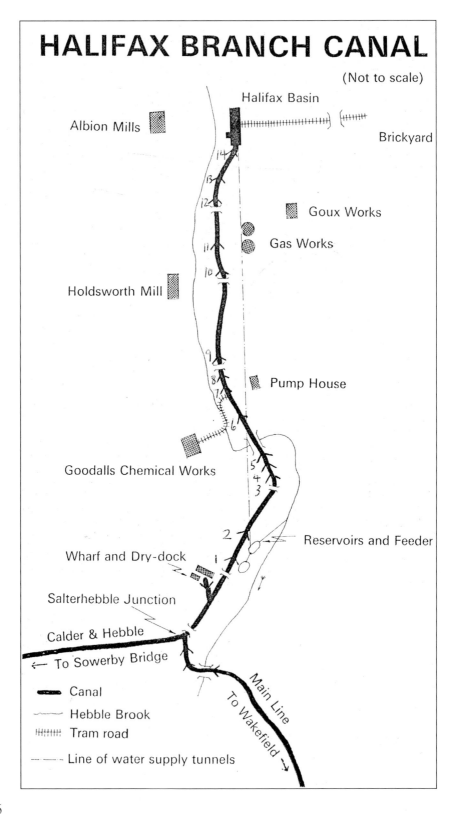

HALIFAX BRANCH CANAL

(Not to scale)

Halifax Basin

Albion Mills

Brickyard

Goux Works

Gas Works

Holdsworth Mill

Pump House

Goodalls Chemical Works

Reservoirs and Feeder

Wharf and Dry-dock

Salterhebble Junction

Calder & Hebble

← To Sowerby Bridge

Main Line
To Wakefield ↘

Canal
Hebble Brook
Tram road
Line of water supply tunnels

A view across lock no.3 of the Halifax Branch's fourteen locks at Siddal, showing the hilly terrain through which it passed.

Canal. Siddal.

Ideally, a canal picture should also feature a boat but such illustrations seem impossible to find for the Halifax Branch. Nonetheless, this attractive postcard view dating from the 1900s, looking down the waterway from above lock no.8 shows the canal in the steep-sided Hebble Valley. (*Trevor Ellis Collection*)

Opposite: The sketch map shows the short and steep Halifax Branch Canal, where tolls were double those applicable on most of the rest of the Calder & Hebble. The pumping station worked round the clock raising water from Salterhebble basin through a 1,170-yard tunnel to the reservoirs from where it was piped into the summit level of the canal. At the Goux Works, 'night soil' collected from the town's privvies was tipped into barges to be carried away to wharves on the Selby Canal and Yorkshire's River Derwent for use as a fertiliser. This traffic continued into the 1920s. (*Peter Spence*)

John Holdsworth & Co.'s worsted spinning mills, founded in 1830 and established above the ninth lock in 1844 had a quarter-mile-long frontage onto the Hebble Brook next to the canal, with over 2,000 employees at one time. Like several canalside factories, it used waterborne coal to generate steam power and even had its own compact gasworks. This is a view of the Shaw Lodge premises looking across the canal, towpath and brook.

This 1940s view looks north into the terminal basin of the Halifax Branch and shows the four-storey stone-built end warehouse with its arch above a channel leading beneath to open water outside the 1879-built Halifax Flour Society's Bailey Hall Mills beyond. John Mackintosh & Sons, manufacturers of 'Rolo' and 'Quality Street', leased Albion Mills at the end of a small arm going off to the left of the picture from 1911 until 1950 and were extensive users of the canal. Patons & Baldwins, the wool company, also had their factory alongside the canal, making extensive use of the wool sheds shown (where the roof extends out over the water). The cooling tower was part of a power station while the nearby loading staithe belonged to a brickworks. (*Peter Spence Collection*)

The main office of the Calder & Hebble was situated at Southgate in the town centre for most of the life of the Halifax Branch but was moved in the 1940s into the canal agent's former premises in the basin adjacent to the end warehouse. The water-served flour mill lies just behind it in this northwards-looking view. This building is still standing and has been incorporated into the present-day Nestle complex. (*Peter Spence Collection*)

Closure of the flour mill in the mid-1930s, when owned by the Cooperative Wholesale Society, seriously affected the Halifax Branch's traffic and it then gradually fell into disuse before abandonment in 1942. The last barge came down in June 1942 and filling-in of the canal began. Mackintoshes (subsequently Rowntree-Mackintosh and now Nestle) took over the mill and most of the basin buildings. On this canal, at least, infilling was realistic, unlike in areas where a waterway is essential to drainage and the drowning of an unsupervised child often produces calls for such a procedure. Tipping is shown taking place at lock no.5 *c*.1950. (*Peter Spence Collection*)

119

Turning left after leaving Salterhebble top lock takes a vessel such as Clegg Brothers' coal-laden *William*, with horse line taut, along the Calder & Hebble main line towards Sowerby Bridge. Horse lines were about 100ft long with a diameter of just over $\frac{1}{2}$in and made of cotton. This newspaper photograph was taken in 1938. Like *George*, shown on page 72, *William* was motorised in 1943 and the two craft were subsequently each worked single-handedly. *Cissie* and *Cresol*, the other two members of the fleet, were then sold along with the two horses.

Alph Sharp & Co.'s Copley chemical works were situated on the northern bank of the Calder & Hebble's summit level. This 1930s advertisement picture shows their wharf with a vessel moored alongside.

Yet another horse-drawn dumb vessel, this time loaded for Sowerby Bridge and posed for the photographer standing on Copley Lane Bridge. In the 1940s and 1950s it was impossible for craft to pass each other between Salterhebble and Sowerby Bridge as the channel had become so silted up and narrow. Fully-loaded motor barges took over two hours to traverse the two miles and there are tales of a captain of one such vessel who regularly entertained a lady friend in the cabin aboard his craft as it made its own way along this stretch, with the tiller unattended and the engine on tick-over.

There was usually a queue of coal-laden craft waiting to be discharged outside the gasworks on the eastern fringe of Sowerby Bridge. The photograph shows the rear of the line of waiting boats in the days between 1901 and 1924 when Albert Wood delivered supplies.

Opposite below: Dumb wooden vessels, including flat-topped tank barges, are shown moored outside Yorkshire Tar Distillers premises at Knottingley in the 1900s. Craft collected tar before the Second World War from gasworks on the Calder & Hebble at Sowerby Bridge, Halifax, Elland, Brighouse, Ravensthorpe and Wakefield to bring to these works for processing.

A view of the head of the queue of craft waiting to discharge at Sowerby Bridge gasworks in the 1930s when Clegg Brothers were responsible for coal deliveries, which they maintained until the gasworks closed in 1954. The tub is poised above *Cresol* with *George* next in line. Both craft were able to bring loads of sixty tons here at this time.

Albert Wood, the canal carrier, designed and built the full length narrowboat (70ft x 7ft) *Reggie* at Point End, Sowerby Bridge, where the Calder & Hebble and Rochdale Canal meet. The vessel was launched in May 1906 and used for trading across the Pennines, via the Rochdale Canal, onto the narrow canals around Manchester. Mr Wood's son, Reggie, felt the vessel was ugly, having, with seven planks, one plank too many. The craft was scrapped in 1923 and the timber obtained from it used to build six rafts.

When originally opened in 1804, the Rochdale Canal immediately attracted extensive grain traffic from Lincolnshire to the rapidly expanding city of Manchester. Abandoned in 1952, the Yorkshire part was restored and reopened in 1996. This photograph, taken in 2001 looking westwards along the line of the Calder & Hebble towards its terminal basin at Sowerby Bridge from the junction of the Calder & Hebble and Rochdale Canal, shows a duck entering the former from the latter and moored pleasure craft.

Opposite below: The Rochdale Canal Co.'s 72ft x 13½ ft Mersey Flat *Primrose* reached Sowerby Bridge in June 1921 and is shown discharging the final bale of its cargo of wool at Lock Hill Mill below the second lock of the Rochdale Canal. The vessel, too large to use the Calder & Hebble, would then set off back across the Pennines. At this time, the canal's draught had decreased from its original 4ft to 3ft and the vessel was carrying only thirty-five tons. One month later, the Rochdale Canal Carrying Co.'s fleet was disbanded, having commenced operation in 1888.

124

The warehouses in the Calder & Hebble's terminal basin and mills alongside the Rochdale Canal at Sowerby Bridge are shown on this early photograph taken from Norland, to the south, in 1865. The Rochdale Canal passes just to the south of the basin, its junction with the Calder & Hebble lying out of shot to the right. The Calder is even closer to the camera on a course almost parallel to the two canals. At this time, the stabling often used for canal horses was beneath Bolton Brow Wesleyan Chapel to the right of the low building in the centre of the photograph.

The Rochdale Canal Co.'s maintenance boat *Engineer* lies moored at Luddenden Foot, a stone-built settlement two miles above Sowerby Bridge. A wharf crane and cargo of stone, lying where it was discharged near a wheelwright's premises, are visible on the towpath side in this 1920s picture looking eastwards.

Opposite top: Regular through traffic using both the Calder & Hebble and Rochdale Canal included salt cake from Little Lever, near Bolton, to Redfearns' glassworks at Barnsley and, in the opposite direction, block salt ex-ship at Hull to Crabtree & Cryer's chemical works on the Rochdale summit pound. Hollidays' chemicals traffic has previously been mentioned on page 75. All these movements would pass through the canal at Hebden Bridge, shown in this westward-facing view of the town lock featuring the Calder aqueduct and former canal warehouses beyond. The very last through cargo on the Rochdale was myrabolams, loaded in Manchester docks for delivery to Dewsbury. It was brought by *Salterhebble*, ex-*Thomas*, in September 1937.

Opposite below: The Rochdale Canal was frequently affected by winter ice and here three of the canal company's craft are trapped in February 1902 below Mill Walk lock, near Oldham, while bound for Sowerby Bridge. Should their cargoes have been destined for Calder & Hebble wharves east of that town, transhipment at Sowerby Bridge into smaller craft would have been necessary. (*Waterways Museum, Goole*)

126

For this picture we return to the Calder & Hebble at Sowerby Bridge basin. During the Second World War, white flour from Canada was imported and delivered to Sowerby Bridge by barge, where it was unloaded and taken to be blended with locally-milled home-grown wheat to produce off-white 'National Flour'. Here in 1943, sacks of this commodity blended at the local C.W.S. mill are being loaded into the Calder Carrying Co.'s *Sowerby Bridge* outside the terminal warehouse, for delivery to Leeds and perhaps transhipment there to a Leeds & Liverpool Canal 'shortboat' for carriage to Skipton. *Sowerby Bridge*, assisted by *Frugality*, brought the last cargo to travel the whole length of the Calder & Hebble to this basin when it delivered woodpulp in September 1955. The terminal warehouse is now a bar and restaurant.